LIFE

A question to ponder & a journey to wander

Sushma Krishnan

Made with ❤ on the BookLeaf Publishing Platform
www.bookleafpub.in
www.bookleafpub.com

Dedication

This book is dedicated to the invisible spark that lit a fire I never knew existed — the spark that awakened my love for poetry, arriving unannounced yet finding me at just the right time.

It all began as a playful response. A fellow Toastmaster, Suresh Kalyanakrishnan, shared a beautiful poem in our group and instead of replying with a simple "well done," I felt a creative nudge to respond — not with praise but with a poem of my own, just four simple lines.

What started as a passing moment became a quiet revelation. Poetry wasn't just something I admired from afar — it was something waiting within me, longing to be found.

Since then, poetry became my language for love, reflection and celebration — a way to honour the special people in my life, capture fleeting thoughts and mark moments too precious to forget.

This journey was never part of any plan, but it gently unfolded into something that now feels like home.

To that **unseen force** — whether fate, chance or something divine — this book belongs to you.

Preface

Poetry has always been my way of capturing emotions, thoughts and fleeting moments that often slip through the cracks of everyday conversation.

There are feelings too subtle for casual words, reflections too personal for loud declarations and experiences too layered to explain in a single breath. Whenever life offers me such moments — the kind that sit heavy on the heart or dance lightly across the mind — poetry steps in as my voice.

This collection is a reflection of those experiences — both deeply personal and universally human — that shape us, mold us and quietly leave their mark, even when we fail to notice.

Each poem carries a piece of my story, but it also holds space for yours. My hope is that, somewhere between these lines, readers find glimpses of their own journeys, their own emotions and their own truths mirrored back at them.

Writing these poems has been a process of self-discovery, healing and expression — a journey of

translating the unspoken into something tangible. And now, sharing them with you completes that circle, making this experience even more meaningful.

Because for me, whatever is difficult to express in straightforward prose often finds its way out through poetry — raw, honest and unfiltered.

Acknowledgements

Crafting poems is one part of the journey, but having people who stand by you and believe in your voice makes all the difference. Thank you Mom, Rekha, Sumanth and Dad for your constant encouragement.

A big thanks to my business partner, Satish Rao, for always standing by me.

Thanks to Ashlesh Rao, whose observation—*"You have a way with words"*—still linger in my mind as a silent motivator.

And to our lovely little princess, Maanvi—your innocent feedback brought so much joy to this process.

Maanvi: *"I like this paragraph very much!"*

Me (curious): *"Why?"*

Maanvi: *"Because it looks like a moral."*

Coming from a 7-year-old... hmmm

Maanvi: *"I don't like this line."*

Me (even more curious): *"Why?"*

Maanvi: *"Because it has the word 'scared.' You should be brave!"*

Thank you for your wisdom, my little critic. You made this journey even more memorable.

1. Life … A Short Word That Has A Long Meaning

"How'z life?" we ask as a conversation starter
"Fine!" will usually be a short & sweet barter
Between the two lies a lot to disclose
Which we do only to those who are close

"How'z life?" such a short question
Has a lot to explore now that I mention
How do you we even begin?
Open the door to the long journey within

"How'z life?" a question to ponder
How deep the answer might be, we wonder
Do we focus only on the splendour?
Or the collection of many a blunder?

"How'z life?" an opportunity to muse
Many an option do we have to choose
Picking one in a bucket of words
Will determine our journey forwards or backwards

"How'z life?" sends a volley of questions
Which makes us experience a hurricane of emotions
The key is how well we balance

While we are on the journey towards acceptance

"How'z life?" an opportunity to introspect
Each of our lives in great depth
Hide & Seek a game which life plays with us
 Answers we find which make us glorious

"How'z life?" a pathway to reflect
Our various areas of neglect
Which might have got blocked
And still remain to be unlocked

"How'z life?" a chance to shape the future
To lay the foundation to make it secure
Which was shaky from the mistakes of the past
To find meaningful solutions which are gonna last

2. The Journey Begins …

The moment we are born starts our journey on Earth
It often starts being in the centre of a circle of mirth
To our parents are we a dream come true
Our colourful journey starts with many a vibrant hue

The colours start changing on each of our life's canvas
Based on the experiences that encompass
We are but an evolving canvas
What we turn into is farther than a wild guess

Splash! Falls the colour on our canvas – Yellow
Curious about everything like a cute little fellow
Wide-eyed and sparkling are our beautiful eyes
Everything around us appears to be somewhat nice

Splash! Falls the colour on our canvas – Green
Starts our learning without us even knowing
Life teaches us step by step
Our pitcher of knowledge starts filling up

Splash! Falls the colour on our canvas – Orange
Setbacks, Disappointments & Challenges – life does arrange
Like broken crayons do we become

How we transform the pieces decides the eventual
outcome

Splash! Falls the colour on our canvas – Red
A transformation of sorts -this is where our life has led
A Version Two do we become – Taller, Stronger &
Sharper
A new challenge ahead for us to conquer

Splash! Falls the colour on our canvas – Blue
Emotional depth & clarity reflects this hue
Our life's evolving canvas does give a clue
On what else is still due

Splash! Falls the last colour on our canvas – Purple
When we are at a stage where life becomes a full circle
Realizing that we are just a dot in the centre
Still a lot to explore in this amazing adventure

3. The People In Our Lives

...

Right from the time we are born
Our lives are shaped by various people who adorn
Like a sculptor who creates magic with clay
These people impact our lives in many a way

From caring hands in the form of parents
Whose unconditional love is very much apparent
To loving hands in the form of grandparents
Who consider us as a golden present

From amazing friends who join hands with us
And never leave us mid-way in any form of crisis
To path-creating mentors who are but a handful
They are the ones who make our lives meaningful

From a few lucky people who become "The One & Only"
Making the lives of their better halves beautiful & jolly
To those who embrace the role of near & dear ones
When challenging situations suddenly stuns

While we are in this bubble of happiness
Like sharp pins do come a few to create a mess
However, it all depends on how we take it

When taken positively, we reach our summit

Introduced are we into a world of jealousy
Being a receiver is absolutely messy
Humiliation, comparison and a dose of insensitiveness
Adds a lot to our emotional stress

"Who needs people?" we start to question
That's the point we need to take a decision
"Who needs **such** people?" a quick reframe
Will fit our happy picture back in the frame

Life is a roller-coaster of ups & downs
People in our lives have already shown
Whom we can trust our heart's wish
They are the ones we need to cherish

4. Failure? Stepping Stone Or An "It's Over" Zone?

How easy it is to tell the word "failure"
If only it's experience is as easy to endure
It takes us through a journey of seven stages
Which in our mind feels like ages

Shock is the first state we are usually thrown in
Leaving our minds in a total spin
Robbed are we of the peace within
We only have to bear it with a grin

Frustration takes over next
Giving our mind absolutely no rest
Being calm is what's needed at best
Whether we can is the absolute test

Doubt then creeps up in absolute silence
Plays around with our mind's utterance
Makes us think "I am not capable"
When in reality the feat ahead is achievable

Fear then blinds us of the clear picture
Now the mind is nothing but a messy mixture
Makes us forget the bravery within

To overcome challenges and win

Reflection now steps in like a flashback
Making our minds rewind things back
What went wrong? Curiosity heightens
Slowly, the clear picture begins to make sense

Adaptation then asks us "See that?"
Making our minds wear a student's hat
Putting us in a winner's mold
Leading us to a strike of gold

Mastery is the final stage
Freeing our minds from failure's cage
Making it a stepping stone to our success
All this while to which we had no access

5. Success – The Mystery Prize

What does success mean to you?
Is a question to which several answers are in queue
It does vary from person to person
Who would have gone through many a long run

Significance is what few people connect with
Adding meaning when they reach the zenith
Silent achievers they generally are
Glowing brightly like the night stars

Understanding is how few define success
Knowledgeable they are in various fields no less
They are a source of answers people can go to
When faced with challenges wondering what to do

Confidence is a form of success
Which many develop for many a conquest
From fear, self-doubt and low self esteem
Climbing the ladder of success to realize their dream

Creativity is what makes few people shine
They are more like a gold mine
In many a way do they make a difference

Creating "out-of-the-box" solutions being their essence

Excellence in whatever they set their hands on
No matter the magnitude on the challenge they take on
This is what few people associate success to
Building credibility as the people to go to

Stability is another way of success
Which many embrace their whole lives no less
This is indeed a tough form of success to achieve
When uncertainty and certainty constantly interweave

Satisfaction is a gem of a success
Which very few have it in them to access
Being satisfied and grateful for what we have
Isn't a piece of cake to halve

6. Thoughts – The Unspoken Messengers

Hither & tither keeps running
All our thoughts in full swing
Not a moment are they quiet
Try & see if you can recollect

Do each thought occur with a purpose?
Or is it just a clever ruse?
We will only know when we dig deeper
We are the ultimate decision-maker

Some thoughts may just be a repeat telecast
Of many a thing that happened in the past
Is it still necessary to keep them in action?
Is the million dollar question

Some thoughts only create fear
Of everything that's far and near
Making us forgo many a dream
That is indeed fear's scheme

Some thoughts paint a picture of happiness
As they are from our life's moments very precious
We tend to linger in them a bit longer

As that's what makes our heart grow fonder

Some thoughts make us way too anxious
As they take us through an unknown abyss
With the unknown future staring at us
Our minds spin like a tornado clueless

Some thoughts open up doors of creativity
That add variety to what we do aplenty
This also brings out our vibrant side
Which all the while was hiding aside

Thoughts in all power up our lives
When we head in a direction that thrives
It's all in our hands or should I say mind?
To ensure that we are not left behind

7. The Past – A House In Our Memory

When you think of the past
Do you think of times you were having a blast?
Good, old memories rekindled
Makes you feel more enkindled

When you think of the past
Of memories which you din't wanna last
You only end up with a heart that's cold
When it should actually be like gold

The past is a mystery
Even though it is your history
The way it keeps bouncing back
Is something that needs some slack

How will you then handle this mystery?
And take charge of your life's victory
That is one of life's greatest challenges
Which will help you through the ages

Some of the past you can choose to ignore
As something not worthy enough to explore
If still not erased by now

Just do it so in a way you know

Some of the past you are struggling with
Needs work at a deeper level beneath
For your mind is an extremely deep well
Layer by layer of memories you will be able to shovel

If not addressed soon enough
It could end up becoming really tough
Work on it before it's too late
You sure do not want it in your plate

Choose the precious memories of the past
That helps to carve a wonderful future that will last
The journey of your past is often too vast
Pick & choose to use it as your life's mast

8. The Present – A Gift To Cherish

Is the present as valuable as they say?
Do you want to check it in your own way?
Let's go on an introspective mode
And find out what's along the road

What defines your present?
A combination of various elements?
Between the recollection of the past
And the future that's going to be vast

You may not have everything
But, you may have enough blessings
As long as you are not living in servitude
It is worth having an attitude of gratitude

You may not be having the best time yet
It does not mean you need to disconnect
From a better future in store
Prepare for it with a mighty roar

Feel that the present is way too challenging?
With the current scenario having no meaning
Remember that you have the fortitude

To stand tall even amidst the challenge's magnitude

The present isn't meant just to spend
It's an opportunity to mend
The many failures that have happened
Because it still isn't the end

The present is a golden opportunity
To create a promising future that 's not empty
Use it wisely to make the most of it
This way, your immediate past also becomes a hit

The present is indeed a gift
Never allow even a moment to drift
The size of the gift may vary
However, it will remain forever in your memory

9. The Future ... A Dream To Nurture

How does the future look like to you?
An optimist says – a myriad of hues
A pessimist says – it looks rather bleak
A realist says – It's something we can tweak

"May you have an awesome future!"
Constantly wish our amazing elders
Is this so-called future already preset
Or is it a path to have our ambitions met?

"Carve your future" the wise ones say
Looks more like a sculptor's way
We will not know the outcome
Till the finishing point does come

"Your future is predestined!" astrologers say
Does it really have to be this way?
"What's in store for us?" we begin to wonder
The answers we start to look yonder

We start to worry about the invisible future
Being anxious becomes our second nature
The future starts to look humongous

Slowly into a deep trench our confidence plunges

Relax! Nobody knows what the future holds
We can only explore what's in it's folds
To create an amazing future, be bold
The result will be it's weight in gold

"I am scared of the future!" is quite natural
Let go of the fear and make it more adventural
Remember you have only one chance
To a promising future that you can enhance

The future is an amazing mystery
Which will become a page in your life's history
Focus on what's in your hands
And see for yourself where you will land!

10. Attitude Is Everything

"Attitude is everything!" they say
Is it more than performance, think you may
Can't having enough talent pave the way
To have success in your sway?

Tenacity is something very powerful
The ability to keep going no matter what pulls
This attitude increases your chances of success
And you will end up moving like a super-fast express

Trust is an amazing factor
Which will eventually matter
Being trustworthy is what people look for
When they reach out to you for a favour

Integrity makes you stand out
Making you get a huge shout-out
As this is indeed a rare quality to have
Reflecting that you are incredibly brave

Thankfulness for what you have
Even though there are a lot of things to crave
Sets you on a path where it truly counts
As having an attitude of gratitude is paramount

Understanding others is a pretty strong trait
That comes only to those who are great
As being empathetic requires a beautiful heart
You may be one such person to impart

Discipline may sound way too strict
But is an attitude to embrace in life's twist
As it keeps you on your winning path
No matter what obstacles come in the aftermath

Enthusiasm is something you need to replenish
As many things in life may not go as per your wish
This attitude ultimately will decide
The overall success in your life's ride

11. Beauty – Lies In Our Own Eyes

Beauty – a very strong word to describe
Something which has the power to mesmerize
Let's try to explore this world
And see what lies in it's folds

Is beauty about appearance?
Yes or No? Tough to take a stance
As beauty isn't just skin-deep
There are several layers within we need to seek

Starts with a beautiful mind
Which pushes all materialism behind
This beauty has a mind of it's own
Which makes it live in a meaningful zone

"One with a pure heart" – are they
Who put others first in their own way
They have a heart of gold
Which glitters beautifully mutlifold

"A gem of a character" – are they
Who wipe other's tears away
Kindness is deeply embedded

Which they show making others feel empowered

"Beauty lies in the eyes of the beholder!" they say
It comes down to how you see it your way
Perceptions play such an important role
In looking for beauty in other souls

Empathy is a mirror of beauty
The beauty of showing kindness as a duty
This quality enhances the way we choose
To see those who step in our shoes

Beauty and the beast – the competitive duo
Are both within ourselves though
It all depends on what we hold dear
When we look into our life's mirror

12. This Way … That Way … Yet Another Way

A coin has two sides on which it can flip
Situations in life have many along the trip
Life isn't as easy as a head or tail
Many a challenge do we need to prevail

In the midst of all these
We often forget about our gift to see
Beyond what is right in front of us
And come to a conclusion thus

We have the gift to perceive
Which opens several doors for us to receive
Learning which we hadn't even imagined
Considering the way our minds were programmed

In tricky situations, our minds trick us even more
Making us blind to certain views we choose to ignore
If only we keep our minds more open
A world of possibilities and truths we will awaken

Why are we hesitant to view differently?
Doesn't it give us much more clarity?
The moment we step into the other person's shoes

We get to experience the real views

A mind shift is what's needed
To start looking from angles not heeded
That's when we get to see the real picture
And be able to find a lasting fixture

How do you now become good at it?
Practice more and you will make it
The deeper you go each time
Makes you be at your prime

Just one life-changing skill
Which can be learnt with your own free will
Is enough to open new doors of understanding
Your views about life thus expanding

13. Emotions – The Never-Ending Ocean …

A day in our life doesn't go by
Without visiting each house nearby
The tenants vary in nature
They still reside no matter your stature

The tenant in the bright coloured house
Is the one to cheerfully rouse
Bring a smile on people's faces when they enjoy
That tenant is none other than Joy

Another tenant is constantly inside
Ever scared to venture outside
Often lives in fear instead of being fearless
That tenant is none other than Uneasiness

There is a house which is so gloomy
As the tenant inside is extremely doomy
Can't blame the poor soul who needs relief
That tenant is none other than Grief

There is a house that's almost drowned
As it's tenant is wallowing trying to find ground
It's not easy as it starts to wilt

That tenant is none other than Guilt

Then there is a house – a pleasant coloured one
It's tenant 's purity is comparable to none
Their presence make things fit like a glove
That tenant is none other than Love

Then there is a house which keeps shaking
As it's tenant heart is constantly quaking
With squeals of enormous merriment
That tenant is none other than Excitement

Finally there is this house which is red
Fuming non-stop where reasoning becomes dead
If not taken care, it's tenant reaches a cruel stage
That tenant is none other than Rage

A day in our life doesn't go by
Without visiting each house nearby
All the tenants live in our own mind
We just need to juggle them like one of a kind

14. Your Mind .... Your Superpower

Jumping from one point to another
Like a trapeze artist comparable to no other
Is a powerhouse lying between our own ears
Guess what it is ...you will have something to cheer

Having many an unexplored territory
Being a target for many a worry
It can be an endless river to ferry
The point is to choose what makes it merry

A bottomless pit it can be from time to time
Left unaddressed, it can be like a slippery slime
Snap out of it, we really must
Else misery will be our permanent guest

Like a garden, we need to nurture
Else disappointingly it can lead to a rupture
What you sow in it is what you reap
Make sure you feed it the best thoughts to keep

Treat it like an open canvas
And the opportunity becomes vast
You can colour it the way you like

Letting go of colours you actually dislike

Give a piece of it to those who play
You will then create your own way
You need to be proud of your own mind
And not allow it to be left behind

Very often, it encounters a tsunami
Stealing your sense of bonhomie
Take care not to get trapped
Else it can put you in a tight wrap

The mind is a way to happiness or woe
You decide to make it your friend or foe
Remember, striking the right balance
Makes it a go-to for the right guidance

15. Mirror, Mirror On The Wall ...

Mirror, mirror on the wall
Who is the most beautiful of us all?
The mirror said "Don't set expectations at all
As they only lead to a great fall"

Mirror, mirror on the wall
Do I look as confident as a lion's call?
The mirror said "Don't focus just on the look
What matters is being confident like a well-read book"

Mirror, mirror on the wall
What shines in me most of all?
The mirror said "The kindness in you glows with warm radiance
It's a quality that shines in brilliance"

Mirror, mirror on the wall
Tired ... do I look about to fall?
The mirror said "Focus on yourself more
There will be a lot of things to explore"

Mirror, mirror on the wall
Can you read my eyes and feel it all?

The mirror said "Your eyes reflect what's deep within
you
Feelings, struggles and challenges that are true"

Mirror, mirror on the wall,
What am I hiding, if anything at all?
The mirror said "Your unspoken fears and desires
That your true self really aspires"

Mirror, mirror on the wall
How do I look like a new person standing tall?
The mirror said "Go and break every wall
That tries to make you fall"

Each and every day, we look into the mirror
Shouldn't each look reflect something to cheer?
It's now your turn to tell the mirror on the wall
"Oh mirror, thanks for it all, now I stand amazing and
tall!"

16. Patterns – Repeat, Repeat & Repeat

It may be your favourite song
But how many times can you listen along?
While this song plays stuck in your head
Patterns play with your life till you are dead

"Is that all?" You may ask
Not until you take the patterns to task
All you have to do is recognize them
You will be on the road to freedom

"What are these patterns?" You might wonder
Habits, thinking or behaviour that lead to blunder
The fact is you may not even be aware
You need to bring them out in the glare

Some may be amazingly funny
Others may make you lose your money
Whatever it is – make sure to take care
Else, you will only end up having an empty stare

Some patterns may be very deep
Unexpectedly, many a time they may creep
The root cause thus needs to be explored

As it isn't something to be ignored

Each pattern has it's own history
You need to unravel it's mystery
Else your peace of mind will become history
You, being unable to gain the much-needed victory

Take a walk down your memory lane
Your efforts will not go in vain
It's better than being stuck in a misery train
Putting unwanted pressure on your brain

The deepest ones will be found
Only when you take on a journey inbound
Answers may be hidden deep in your subconscious
This journey is going to be very precious

17. Upbringing – What You Sow Is What You Reap

Imagine making a sculpture
Trying to create an amazing structure
The end result is a reflection
Of your efforts, love and passion

When a small sculpture demands so much
Just imagine creating a gem out of a person as such
Well, it starts right from home
A life-lesson learning dome

Then comes our system of education
Which molds us into builders of our nation
Unlucky are we if it only meant greater a grade
Growing up not being able to call a spade as a spade

Then comes the environment we are exposed to
It indeed has a lot to do
Surrounded by positive people is a gift
Else, consider giving such a company a drift

Our culture is the central compass
Which shows us the direction towards success
It's important that we follow the direction

As this is to our success - the very foundation

Then comes the scary part
Where many try to tear our dreams apart
In the name of society, we are often misled
When in reality, the right guidance needs to be spread

Then comes the most valuable protector
It's our life's most important director
The values which we imbibe and stand for
Will take us in the true sense, very far

All of the above put together
Has the impact to influence one another
Upbringing thus plays a crucial role
In the journey of our lives as a whole

18. The Difficulty Of Being Honest

One of the questions we cannot ignore
Which even today is a tricky one to explore
"Is it good to be honest?"
"Will it even fetch a great harvest?"

"Honesty is the best policy"
We were taught since our infancy
"Is it really so?" we started doubting it
As we grew up and like a hard cork ball did it hit

Day in and day out, we got to see
Honesty in many a degree
Which makes us wonder what's actually right
Because what we get to see isn't a pretty sight

Some degree of dishonesty is okay
Say some people who think they have a say
Yes, it's fine as long as it's a white lie
To save someone who will otherwise die

However, if white lies are given a different colour
To get things done in their favour
That wont be fair to the couth

Who still stick to the truth

Only a handful of people abide by the truth
To gauge their action, you don't need a sleuth
They are so strong within
That even tough situations do not pull them in

Our entire life is a test of honesty
Which we need to live with a no-lies policy
A liar can easily build a dynasty
Which comes crashing down due to it's monstrosity

Last but not the least, they say
"Satyameva Jayate!" – let this be your way
Follow it with all your heart
You will be blessed with a beautiful life no matter what

19. Regret – A Place Not So Pleasant

This is a place we often go to
Not willingly but as a have-to
It is the place called regret
Found in everyone's lives no matter how it is set

It takes us through a sight-seeing tour
Long and winding with a lot of detours
We need to take that trip no matter what
It's a way of letting go of the past

Reproach is often one of the stops
In this trip where our pasts are the hosts
Enough of blaming oneself is the lesson
Of this trip as part of your learning mission

Emptiness is a spot which one cant fill
Having the weight of a hill
The spot which made us miss many a chance
If only we had another opportunity to enhance

Guilt keeps reminding us
Of the numerous mistakes tremendous
It's like getting stuck in a whirlpool

Which is as stubborn as a mule

Rejection keeps haunting thus
Especially when it happens from us
Making it hard to forgive ourselves
Even as time goes by nevertheless

Erosion takes over, not that of soil
But of our own confidence in turmoil
The key is to bring it to a boil
And not to let all our efforts to foil

Tension keeps building its mansion
When not addressed in this situation
Let regret be a temporary place you visit
When it's needed in life as a fix-it

20. The Other Side Of You

Like a coin that has two sides
Many a time, you may have to flip the tide
In circumstances where your success could derail
You need to decide – head or tail

That decision comes from the strength within
As an unknown task master lies therein
It is none other than your own "the other side"
Which all this while played Seek & Hide

Like an invisible force you din't even know about
It is an amazing one – have no doubt
You just need to recognize it when it comes
And you will get to see for yourself – the outcome

How do you bring out this force, you may ask
Well, that's quite a challenging task
As it needs a deeper exploration
Deep dive into the world of self-revelation

When you start going deeper
Mysteries start coming up and over
You will be surprised to know about your own self
The part you had not explored like a hidden book-shelf

Your life's pages have a lot to tell you
About what is still in your future – due
It sets the foundation for your second innings
Which will lead to more and better winnings

The "other side of you" is often hidden
You may not even know it isn't forbidden
The hesitation to explore this side of you
Could make you lose out on opportunities quite a few

Having the awareness now to explore
Go ahead with a mighty roar
Your life now may not be the last mile
The "other side of you" will make it worthwhile

21. Happy Birthday To You!

All this while, I wrote about life when alive
My views and experiences summed up in a hive
For the reader that's you who is helping me thrive
Let's complete this small poetic journey with a huge
high-five

By now, you may be wondering about the title
How does it make sense in the whole cycle?
Now, my friend I will share
Why I chose this title for a poem so rare

"Happy birthday to you!" is sung every year
To remind that there is still a lot to cheer
Every birthday, remember this point
That this year isn't going to be the endpoint

Each year is like a milestone
Though you may not have reached the throne
Keep trying for what you intend to achieve
For a beautiful purpose which you do believe

Your past is more in shades of black and white
Your future can be amazingly bright
For that you need to take charge of the present

Which is your superpower to make life excellent

Celebrate each year with those you love the most
Make sure you are the perfect host
It's not for any frivolous party
It's only to make the moments more hearty

Let your birthday be an occasion to remember
That you need to slow down when the light shows amber
Slowing down to savour the moment
Before picking up speed for your life's next event

Each year is an add-on to your life
Be grateful for each added moment without strife
Embrace each challenge with all your heart
Life is a gift to be cherished before you depart

Happy Birthday To You! Every
Moment Counts!

www.ingramcontent.com/pod-product-compliance
Lightning Source LLC
LaVergne TN
LVHW050941200726

843508LV00011B/2408